How to use this book

Matched to the National Curriculum, this Collins  is designed to improve spelling skills.

Handy tips included throughout.

Questions split into three levels of difficulty – Challenge 1, Challenge 2 and Challenge 3 – to help progression.

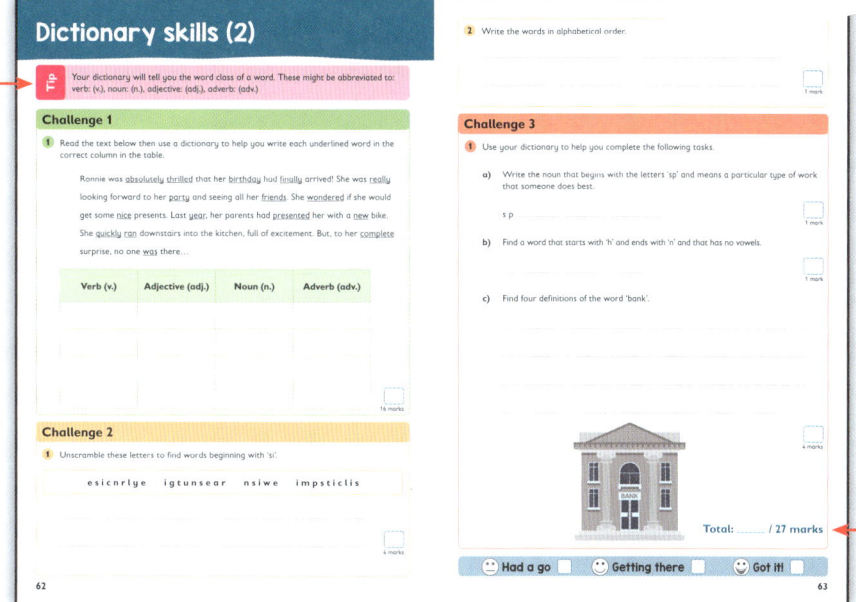

Teaching notes to guide you through some of the key aspects of spelling.

Total marks boxes for recording progress and **'How am I doing?'** checks for self-evaluation.

Starter test recaps skills covered in Year 4.

Four **Progress tests** included throughout the book for ongoing assessment and monitoring progress.

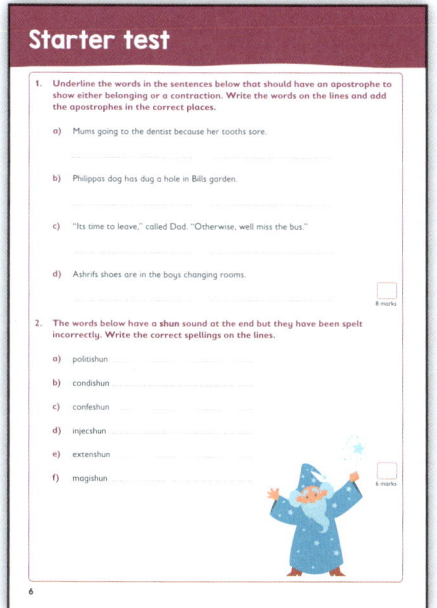

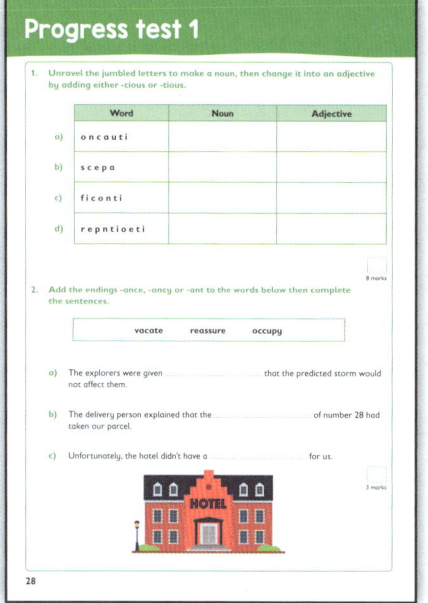

Answers provided for all the questions.

1

Contents

Practising spelling at home	4
Starter test	6
Endings which sound like **shus** spelt -cious	12
Endings which sound like **shus** spelt -tious	14
Endings which sound like **shul** spelt -cial and -tial	16
The endings -ant, -ance and -ancy	18
The endings -ent, -ence and -ency	20
The endings -able and -ible	22
The endings -ably and -ibly	24
Word games (1)	26
Progress test 1	28
The letter string 'ough'	32
Silent letters	34
Apostrophes for possession	36
Apostrophes for contraction	38
Using hyphens	40
Adding suffixes beginning with vowels to words ending in -fer	42
Dictionary skills (1)	44
Word games (2)	46
Progress test 2	48
Words with 'ei' and 'ie'	52
Adding the suffixes -ate, -ise and -ify to make verbs	54
Adding the suffix -en to make verbs	56
Homophones and near-homophones (1)	58
Homophones and near-homophones (2)	60

Dictionary skills (2)	62
Tricky plurals	64
Word games (3)	66
Progress test 3	**68**
Words with unspoken sounds and syllables	72
Prefixes	74
Word families	76
Dictionary skills (3)	78
Tricky words (1)	80
Tricky words (2)	82
Tricky words (3)	84
Word games (4)	86
Progress test 4	**88**
Answers	92

Acknowledgements

The author and publisher are grateful to the copyright holders for permission to use quoted materials and images. All illustrations and images are ©Shutterstock.com and ©HarperCollins*Publishers* Ltd.

Published by Collins
An imprint of HarperCollins*Publishers*
1 London Bridge Street
London SE1 9GF

HarperCollins*Publishers*
Macken House, 39/40 Mayor Street Upper,
Dublin 1, D01 C9W8, Ireland

© HarperCollins*Publishers* Limited 2024

ISBN 978-0-00-862712-6

First published 2024

10 9 8 7 6 5 4 3 2 1

All rights reserved. No part of this publication may be reproduced, stored in a retrieval system, or transmitted, in any form or by any means, electronic, mechanical, photocopying, recording or otherwise, without the prior permission of Collins.

British Library Cataloguing in Publication Data.

A CIP record of this book is available from the British Library.

Publisher: Jennifer Hall
Author: Shelley Welsh
Project Leaders: Richard Toms and Shelley Teasdale
Editorial: Fiona Watson
Cover Design: Sarah Duxbury
Inside Concept Design and Page Layout: Ian Wrigley
Production: Bethany Brohm
Printed in India by Multivista Global Pvt. Ltd

This book is produced from independently certified FSC™ paper to ensure responsible forest management.

For more information visit: www.harpercollins.co.uk/green

Practising spelling at home

In Year 5, children's spelling skills and physical handwriting skills continue to develop. As they read longer, more complex texts and become increasingly independent readers, they will be exposed to a wider range of vocabulary and more challenging spellings.

Having good spelling skills helps children write more fluently as they do not need to spend too long considering how each word is spelt. In turn, they will have the confidence to make more adventurous vocabulary choices and to develop their reading skills in using a dictionary to check for spelling accuracy and word meaning.

Supporting your child

When supporting your child at home, draw their attention to spelling patterns. These might be sound or letter patterns, grammar patterns or word families. It is important to remember that although there are many spelling rules, there are also many words that are exceptions to any obvious rule or pattern. These words just have to be learned.

Your child's vocabulary can be extended by actively engaging in conversation with you and other adults, and by reading a range of genres independently. Encourage your child to be curious about vocabulary, its meaning and how it is spelt. Discussing what your child has been reading, watching on television or listening to on the radio or in podcasts will help develop their vocabulary and their understanding of grammar, as well as their ability to access other areas of the curriculum.

There are many ways that your child can practise spelling at home, independently and with support, and there are a range of practical activities that you might do with your child.

Look, cover, write, check

Look, cover, write, check is a strategy taught in schools which can also be used at home. Write the words your child is learning in the first column of a three- or four-column table. Ask your child to look at the spelling, cover it, write the spelling in the next column then uncover the original spelling to check if they have got it right. The additional blank columns can be used for corrections or extra practice.

Flash cards

Create a double set of the words your child finds tricky to spell. They pick up two cards at a time until they find a pair. Ask them to spell the word out to you verbally.

Word searches and crossword puzzles

There are internet sites for both these activities, as well as many printed books and magazines.

Tic Tac Toe

Create a 'noughts and crosses' grid and provide your child and another player with a face-down pile of the words they are learning and a different colour marker for each player. Players take it in turns to choose a spelling from the pile, read it, memorise the spelling, then write it in one of the grid spaces. The winner is the first to get three-in-a-row correctly spelt words.

Computer or tablet

Give your child the opportunity to type the words they are learning and to experiment with text fonts, sizes and colours.

Creating a good learning environment

As children learn best when they do not feel under pressure, distracted or tired, it is important that your child is:

- positive
- comfortable about making mistakes
- not rushed
- in a quiet, calm working place
- encouraged to check their work.

The importance of reading

Finally, encourage your child to read, read, read! Not only does reading improve their spelling and vocabulary, it stimulates their imagination and is a relaxing pastime in the midst of busy lives too often dominated by screens. Reading is more than just a skill and the impact of *reading for pleasure* should never be underestimated.

Starter test

1. **Underline the words in the sentences below that should have an apostrophe to show either belonging or a contraction. Write the words on the lines and add the apostrophes in the correct places.**

    a) Mums going to the dentist because her tooths sore.

        ....

    b) Philippas dog has dug a hole in Bills garden.

        ....

    c) "Its time to leave," called Dad. "Otherwise, well miss the bus."

        ....

    d) Ashrifs shoes are in the boys changing rooms.

        ....

    8 marks

2. **The words below have a shun sound at the end but they have been spelt incorrectly. Write the correct spellings on the lines.**

    a) politishun ....

    b) condishun ....

    c) confeshun ....

    d) injecshun ....

    e) extenshun ....

    f) magishun ....

    6 marks

3. Write the homophones that are the answers to these clues.

a) Tiny droplets of water in the air, like a light fog.

....

b) The past tense of the verb 'miss'.

....

c) A small, round fruit that grows on a bush or tree.

....

d) A dog might do this with its bone.

....

4 marks

4. Change these adjectives into adverbs by adding the suffix -ly.

a) hungry → ....

b) final → ....

c) simple → ....

3 marks

5. Write the contracted form of the words in bold.

a) **We have** not seen Ben for a few weeks. Perhaps **he has** not been well.

....

b) "I **shall not** be going to that café again," said Mum. "**It is** awful!"

....

c) "**There is** no point in moaning about the weather," said Jack. "You **cannot** change it."

....

d) **Dad has** hung out the washing but I think **it will** rain soon.

....

8 marks

6. Add a suffix to each of the following words to complete the sentences.

| nasty | gentle | regular | possible |

a) Mum goes .... to a physiotherapist.

b) Tia is .... going to live abroad for a year.

c) The bully spoke .... to the new pupil.

d) The mare .... licked her new foal.

4 marks

8

7. Add a prefix to each of these words.

   a) .... s t a r   b) .... p i l o t

   c) .... m e r g e   d) .... s e p t i c

   4 marks

8. Write the words in bold in the passage below in the correct column in the table.

   We've been visiting the Lake District for years. **It's Mum's** favourite place in the world. **She's** a keen hiker and loves the stunning views. Last time, **we'd** just started to walk down Scafell (one of the **area's** most challenging mountains) when **Mum's** ankle started to throb. **She'd** hurt it earlier when my **sister's** hat blew away and she ran after it! Luckily, there was a First Aid kit in **Dad's** car and he bandaged her ankle.

Apostrophe to show a contraction	Apostrophe to show possession

   10 marks

9. Add the suffix -ation to the following verbs to make nouns.

   a) prepare ....

   b) condemn ....

   c) sense ....

   d) assign ....

   4 marks

9

10. **Choose the correct spelling of the adjectives made with the suffix -ous. Write the correct spelling on the line.**

    a) courage → courageous / couragous ....

    b) vigour → vigourous / vigorous ....

    c) court → courteous / courtious ....

    d) humour → humourous / humorous ....

    4 marks

11. **Use the clues to find words which end with a k sound or a hard g sound.**

    a) I am a very old and valuable object. I am of French origin and I end with a **k** sound.

    I am an ....

    b) I am one-of-a-kind and quite special. I am also of French origin and end with a **k** sound.

    I am ....

    c) I am a moveable body part used for tasting, eating and speaking. I am also of French origin but I end with a hard **g** sound.

    I am a ....

    3 marks

10

12. **Complete each sentence with a noun made from the verbs below.**

> invade   collide   divide

a) Stef wrote a story called *The* .... *of the Aliens*.

b) We have multiplication and .... calculations for homework.

c) There was a .... between Frank and Eddie in the playground.

3 marks

13. **Complete each sentence by adding a suffix to each verb below.**

> begin   forgot   prefer

a) We have .... to invite Jude to the party.

b) I have always .... fruit to vegetables.

c) Sofie is .... to understand the French language.

3 marks

Total: _____ / 64 marks

Endings which sound like shus spelt -cious

Teaching note: Some nouns that have been changed into adjectives have an ending that sounds like **shus** spelt -cious. This is usually the case where the root word ends in -ce. For example, vice → vicious.

Challenge 1

Tip: A **mnemonic** is a memory tool that can help you remember how to spell tricky words or letter strings. For example, the letter string -cious can be remembered as '**C**athy **i**s **o**ften **u**ltra **s**mart'.

1. Think of a mnemonic that will help you remember the order of the letters in the ending -cious.

   c ...cats...

   i ...in...

   o ...our...

   u ...underpants...

   s ...scratch...

1 mark

Challenge 2

1. Choose the correct word from the box to complete each sentence.

   | vicious | delicious | gracious | precious |

   a) Dad cooked a ...delicious... meal.

   b) Gran said her wedding ring was very ...precious...

   c) The beast bared its ...vicious... fangs.

12

d) The ballerina received her bouquet with a ...... *gracious* ...... curtsey.

4 marks

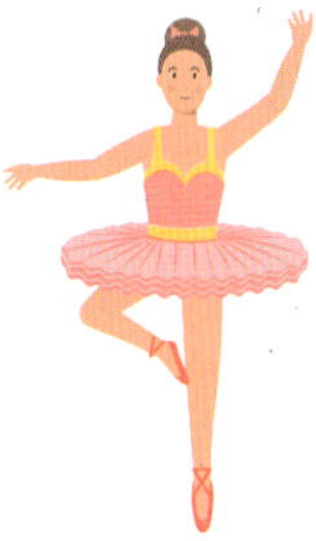

Challenge 3

Teaching note: A **synonym** is a word that has the same or a similar meaning as another word. An **antonym** is a word that has an opposite meaning to another word.

1 Write a definition, an antonym and a synonym for the word **suspicious**. Use your dictionary to help you. Then write the word in a sentence.

Definition: *a feeling or causing suspicion*

Antonym:

Synonym:

In a sentence:

suspicious

5 marks

Total: ____ / 10 marks

Endings which sound like shus spelt -tious

Teaching note: Some nouns that have been changed into adjectives have an ending that sounds like **shus** spelt -tious. For example, ambition → ambitious.

Challenge 1

1. Say the following words out loud. Write the word, marking the syllable breaks with a vertical line. Now write the word again. One has been done for you.

   ambitious   *am | bi | tious*   ambitious

   a) infectious ....

   b) cautious ....

   c) nutritious ....

   d) fictitious ....

   4 marks

Challenge 2

1. Use the words from Challenge 1 (including the example) to complete these sentences.

   a) The rumours about our teacher getting married turned out to be

   ....

   b) We are always very .... when we cross the road outside our school.

   c) My uncle is a determined and .... businessman.

14

d) Fruit and vegetables are an important part of a

.... diet.

e) On his return from the rainforest, Archie discovered he had an

.... disease.

5 marks

Challenge 3

1 Unscramble the letters then use your dictionary to write a definition for each one.

> f u s r a c t i o   s t i o c r u m p u s
>
> p r e u s t e n t i o

....

....

....

6 marks

Total: _____ / 15 marks

Had a go ☐   Getting there ☐   Got it! ☐

15

Endings which sound like shul spelt -cial and -tial

Teaching note: The ending -cial is common after a vowel and the ending -tial is common after a consonant. For example, special and partial.

Challenge 1

1. These words have been written with the wrong endings. Use your dictionary to help you write the correct spellings on the lines.

   a) artifitial ....

   b) spetial ....

   c) substancial ....

   d) parcial ....

   e) essencial ....

   5 marks

Challenge 2

1. Change these nouns into adjectives. Remember, not all words follow the spelling rule! Use your dictionary to check if you need to.

   a) face ....

   b) commerce ....

   c) society ....

   d) confidence ....

   4 marks

Challenge 3

1 Match the words with their definitions then write a sentence containing each word.

> beneficial   glacial   racial

a) ....

   Definition: An unfriendly atmosphere or something produced by ice.

   Sentence: ....

   ....

b) ....

   Definition: Something that improves someone's life.

   Sentence: ....

   ....

c) ....

   Definition: Relating to someone's race.

   Sentence: ....

   ....

9 marks

Total: _____ / 18 marks

Had a go ☐   Getting there ☐   Got it! ☐

17

The endings -ant, -ance and -ancy

Teaching note: If there is a related word with an **ah** or an **ay** sound in the penultimate syllable, -ant, -ance or -ancy are used. For example, subst**a**ntial → subst**ance**. Words with an -ation ending are often a clue. For example, toler**a**tion → toler**ant**. There are many words where the spelling guidance does not help. They just have to be learned!

Challenge 1

1 Add the ending -ant or -ance to each word below, then complete the sentences.

| guide | observe | tolerate | disturb |

a) The night-time .... from our neighbour's party meant we had a bad night's sleep.

b) Our teacher is usually .... of our chattering but today he asked us to work quietly.

c) Polly, who is very ...., spotted the suspicious character instantly.

d) We were given .... on how to conduct the science experiment.

4 marks

Challenge 2

1. Unscramble the letters to complete the words in the grid that end in -ant, -ance or -ancy.

cyhitaesn   cansrureaes   cavancy
stanince   luctarent   upoccant

a) h
b) r
c) v
d) i
e) r
f) o

6 marks

Challenge 3

1. Find the **six** incorrectly spelled words in the box and write them correctly on the lines below.

expectant   agent   pregnent   expectancy
agency   substence   buoyancy   redundancy
tolerance   redundent   infency
reassurence   buoyant   expectence

6 marks

Total: _____ / 16 marks

Had a go ☐   Getting there ☐   Got it! ☐

The endings -ent, -ence and -ency

Teaching note: After a soft **c** sound, a soft **g** sound or **qu**, use -ent, -ence or -ency. For example, frequent → frequency. Once again, there are many words where the spelling guidance does not help. They just have to be learned!

Challenge 1

1 Decide whether to use the ending -ent or -ant with the following word beginnings.

a) frequ..............   b) intellig..............

c) domin..............   d) rec..............

e) occup..............   f) assist..............

6 marks

Challenge 2

1 Complete the words with the endings -ence or -ency.

The boss was impressed at Jack's compet.................... after just

two weeks. His confid.................... and transpar.................... were

refreshing qualities, as was the eloqu.................... of his speech.

4 marks

20

Challenge 3

1 Change the nouns into adjectives and match them to their definitions. Then write a sentence containing each word.

> violence   emergence   fluency

a) ....

Definition: An adjective describing something that is becoming powerful or coming into existence.

Sentence: ....

....

b) ....

Definition: An adjective describing physical force which can cause injury.

Sentence: ....

....

c) ....

Definition: An adjective that describes someone who can speak a language easily and correctly.

Sentence: ....

....

9 marks

Total: _____ / 19 marks

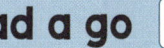 Had a go ☐   Getting there ☐   Got it! ☐

The endings -able and -ible

Teaching note: As with -ant, -ance and -ancy, the -able ending is used if there is a related word ending in -ation. The -able ending is more common than -ible. The -ible ending is common if a complete root word can't be heard before it. For example, horror → horrible. But it can sometimes occur when a complete root word **can** be heard!

Challenge 1

1. Change the words below into adjectives which end in either -able or -ible. Then complete the sentences.

adoration   sense   application   horror

   a) The .... smell in the shed turned out to be a dead mouse.

   b) Lena was falling in love with Magda's .... new puppy.

   c) Finn knew it would be .... to study for the history test.

   d) The teacher's cross words were .... to only a few noisy pupils.

   4 marks

Teaching note: If the -able ending is added to a word ending in -ce or -ge, the 'e' after the 'c' or 'g' must be retained to keep their sounds soft.

Challenge 2

1 Choose the correct spelling from the words in bold and write it on the line.

a) There was a **noticable / noticeable** change in Hallie's mood after her cat went missing.

  ....

b) We thought the long division calculations were almost **impossible / impossable** but our teacher helped us.

  ....

c) Although the weather was very **changeable / changable**, we had a great camping trip.

  ....

d) As the bus came down the hill, the children cheered as the sea became **visable / visible**.

  ....

4 marks

Challenge 3

1 Unscramble the letters to find words ending in -able or -ible. Write the words correctly on the lines.

a) s p b o s e i l   ....

b) l e d u e r n d a s t a n b   ....

c) s b e e n s i l   ....

d) d e e p e b l n d a   ....

4 marks

Total: _____ / 12 marks

Had a go ☐   Getting there ☐   Got it! ☐

23

The endings -ably and -ibly

Teaching note: The endings -ably and -ibly are used to create adverbs. The same spelling rules apply as for the endings -able and -ible.

Challenge 1

1. Find the **four** incorrectly spelt words in the box and write them correctly on the lines below.

conceiveably	considerably	unforgetably
comfortably	noticably	tolerably
agreably	reasonably	applicably

   ....

   ....

   ....

   ....

   4 marks

Teaching note: If the endings -able or -ably are added to words ending in 'y', the 'y' is changed to 'i' in accordance with the spelling rule.

Challenge 2

1. Add the ending -ably to the following words.

   a) vary ....   b) rely ....

   c) pity ....   d) deny ....

   4 marks

24

Challenge 3

1 Unscramble the letters to complete the words in the grid that end in -ably or -ibly.

iybisvl   recydibinl   nbogwlekydeal
hablncgeay   yirepllacreab   hriyborl

a) v
b) i
c) k
d) c
e) i
f) h

6 marks

2 Write the words you have made in alphabetical order on the lines below.

....

....

....

....

....

....

1 mark

Total: _____ / 15 marks

Had a go ☐   Getting there ☐   Got it! ☐

25

Word games (1)

Challenge 1

1) Find at least two other words in the words below. One has been done for you. The order of the letters cannot be changed.

Word	Shorter words within the words
monument	on, me, men
a) inoperable	
b) opportunity	
c) hindrance	
d) cemetery	

8 marks

Challenge 2

1) Move one letter from the five-letter word and add it to the three-letter word to make two new four-letter words. The order of the letters cannot be changed. For example, brave, are → rave, bare.

a) could   for   ....

b) solid   pad   ....

c) hedge   pit   ....

d) house   sit   ....

e) climb   are   ....

10 marks

26

Challenge 3

1 Choose **two** words (one from each group) that make a compound word when put together. The word from the first group comes first in the answer.
Write the compound word on the line.

   a) (day, month, week)   (stop, finish, end)

   ....

   b) (air, vapour, water)   (fall, stumble, trip)

   ....

   c) (car, bus, boat)   (field, park, forest)

   ....

   d) (trousers, jacket, suit)   (container, box, case)

   ....

   4 marks

2 Write the word that completes a third pair of words using the same pattern as the first two pairs. The first one has been done for you.

   pest → pester   jump → jumper   read → *reader*

   a) dove → dive   hove → hive   love → ....

   b) raw → war   live → evil   knits → ....

   c) snip → nips   spin → pins   slot → ....

   3 marks

Total: _____ / 25 marks

Had a go   Getting there   Got it!

27

Progress test 1

1. **Unravel the jumbled letters to make a noun, then change it into an adjective by adding either -cious or -tious.**

	Word	Noun	Adjective
a)	o n c a u t i		
b)	s c e p a		
c)	f i c o n t i		
d)	r e p n t i o e t i		

8 marks

2. **Add the endings -ance, -ancy or -ant to the words below then complete the sentences.**

> vacate   reassure   occupy

a) The explorers were given .... that the predicted storm would not affect them.

b) The delivery person explained that the .... of number 28 had taken our parcel.

c) Unfortunately, the hotel didn't have a .... for us.

3 marks

28

3. **Choose the correct spelling of the words in bold. Write the correct word on the line below each sentence.**

   a) The furious thief protested his **innocence / innocance**.

   ....

   b) The **frequency / frequancy** of flash flooding in our area has become a major concern.

   ....

   c) Bill spoke with great **confidance / confidence** in the inter-house debating competition.

   ....

   3 marks

4. **Add an ending that sounds like shul to change these nouns into adjectives.**

   a) office   ....

   b) commerce   ....

   c) part   ....

   d) essence   ....

   4 marks

5. **Change these words into adjectives by adding an ending that sounds like shus. Match the adjectives with their definitions, then write a sentence containing each word.**

| ferocity | suspect | grace |

a) ....

Definition: Not trusting of someone or something.

Sentence: ....

....

b) ....

Definition: Very fierce and violent.

Sentence: ....

....

c) ....

Definition: Well-mannered and pleasant.

Sentence: ....

....

9 marks

30

6. Answer the clues to complete the words in the crossword which end in -cial, -ance, -ancy, -ency, -tious or -cious.

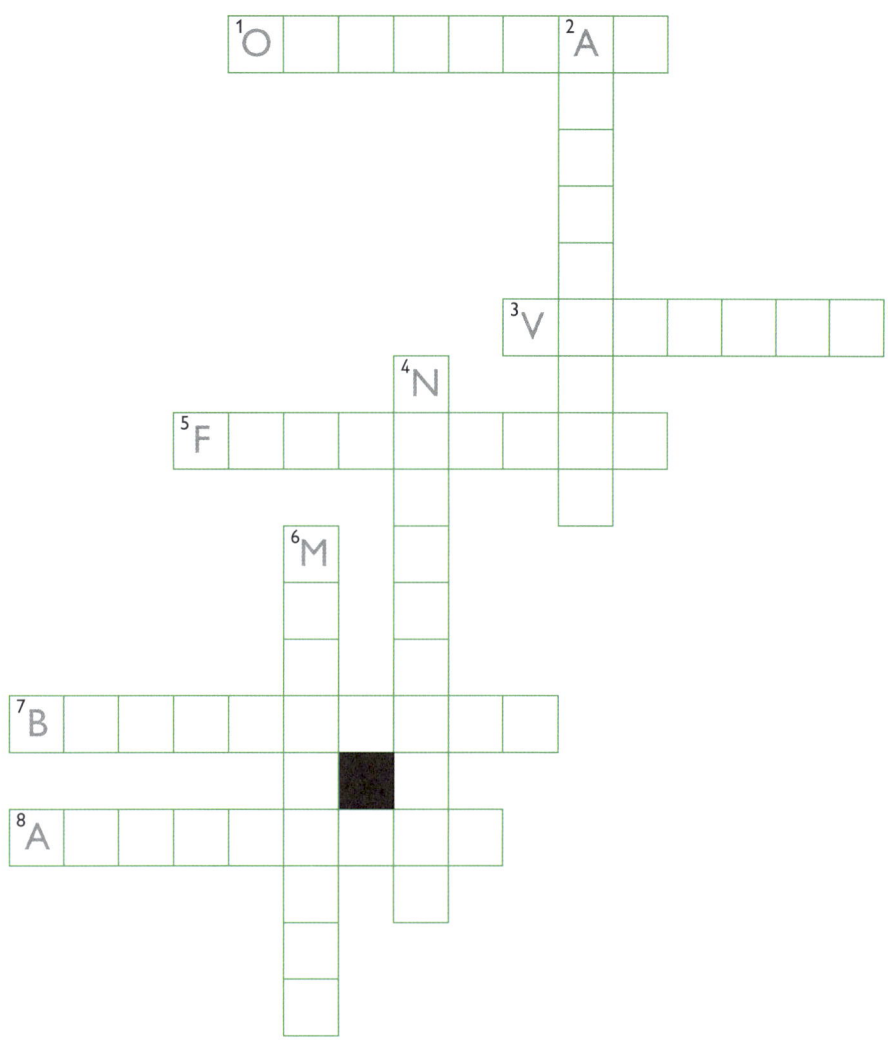

Across
1. Approved by the government or someone in authority
3. A job or position that has not been filled
5. The number of times an event happens during a particular period
7. Describes something that helps people or improves their lives
8. Someone who has a strong desire to be successful, rich or powerful

Down
2. A promise or guarantee made to make someone feel less worried
4. Describes food which helps your body to be healthy
6. Spiteful or vicious

8 marks

Total: _____ / 35 marks

The letter string 'ough'

> **Tip** The letter string 'ough' can be used for a number of different sounds.

Challenge 1

1. Think of a mnemonic that will help you remember the order of the letters in the letter string 'ough'.

    o ....

    u ....

    g ....

    h ....

1 mark

Challenge 2

1. Two words in each sentence have been spelt incorrectly. Write the correct spellings on the line below each sentence.

    a) The ferry crossing was very ruff even thow the wind had died down.

    ....

    b) Dad bawt some tuff thread to sew a button on my cuff.

    ....

    c) The farmer used a plow which made furrows – shallow troffs – in the field, ready for planting seeds.

    ....

32

d) Gran said I'd had enuff coff medicine and that I should drink lots of water.

....

8 marks

Challenge 3

1 Group the words below according to the sound that their 'ough' letter string makes.

enough	although	bough	tough	brought
thought	dough	plough	fought	trough
though	bought	cough	ought

long o sound	aw sound	uff sound	off sound	ow sound

14 marks

Total: _____ / 23 marks

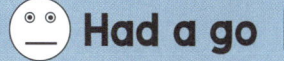 Had a go   Getting there   Got it!

33

Silent letters

Tip: Learn how to spell words with silent letters by stressing the silent letter. For example, pronounce the letter 'd' in the word 'Wednesday' to remind you to include it when writing it.

Tip: The letters b, g, h and k can be silent.
Silent 'b' is almost always at the end of a word, as part of the grapheme 'mb'. Silent 'g' is usually followed by 'n'. Silent 'h' is partnered with other letters, particularly 'w' and 'r'. Silent 'k' is always at the beginning of a word and is followed by 'n'.

Challenge 1

1) Solve the following riddles. The answers all have a silent letter.

   a) I am a quadrilateral with four equal sides, no right angles and two pairs of parallel lines.

      I am a ………………………………………….

   b) I am a flat piece of metal or plastic with teeth. You use me to tidy your hair.

      I am a ……………………….

   c) I am a joint where your finger joins your hand.

      I am a ………………………………………….

   d) I am an imaginary creature with a beard and a pointed hat.

      I am a ……………………………….

   4 marks

Tip: The letters d, l, n and s can be silent.

Challenge 2

1 Find the incorrectly spelt words in the passage and write them correctly on the lines below.

> Last autum, we went to an iland just off the coast of Scotland. We stopped for a picnic when we were hafway there. We had sanwiches and squash. In the field next to us, some newborn caves frolicked with their mothers. We got back in the car and my sister and I taked excitedly all the way to our destination.

....

....

6 marks

Tip: The letters p, t and c can be silent.

Challenge 3

1 Complete each sentence with a word that contains a silent p, t or c.

a) Kai let out a loud .... and his dog came running.

b) Faye started her careful .... up the climbing wall.

c) The shopkeeper gave Ushma a .... for her purchase.

3 marks

Total: _____ / 13 marks

- 😐 Had a go ☐
- 🙂 Getting there ☐
- 😃 Got it! ☐

35

Apostrophes for possession

Teaching note

An apostrophe can be used to show that something belongs to someone or something. The apostrophe is placed:
- between the final letter of the word and the letter 's' in singular nouns
- immediately after the 's' in plural nouns ending in 's'
- between the final letter and the letter 's' in irregular plural nouns.

To show that something belongs to more than one person or thing, the apostrophe is placed after the 's' in the plural word.

Challenge 1

1. The apostrophes in two words in each sentence have been placed incorrectly. Write the words correctly on the lines.

   a) The team gathered in the mens' changing rooms to receive their coachs' praise after their skilful performance.

   ....

   b) The princes' speech, which he made from the castles' balcony, was received with rapturous applause.

   ....

   c) The childrens' dog fell into the pond but the park keepers' quick-thinking meant he was able to rescue her.

   ....

   d) Brittanys' mum, who is a florist, delivered flowers for my grans' birthday.

   ....

   8 marks

36

Challenge 2

1 Select the word that has been written correctly from the words in bold.
Write the correct words on the lines.

> J.B. Arkwright & Sons
>
> Our **boy's / boys'** shoe department has a wide range of state-of-the art trainers at competitive prices. We offer an expert fitting service so you can be confident your **child's / childs'** footwear is the right size.
>
> Our **company's / companys'** aim is to deliver a high level of customer service and we sincerely hope you will become one of **Arkwrights' / Arkwright's** loyal customers.

....

....

4 marks

Teaching note: For proper nouns ending in 's', an apostrophe is placed after the final 's'; sometimes this is followed by another 's' but not always. For example, Jess's kitten / Jess' kitten.

Challenge 3

1 Underline the words in the sentences below that should have an apostrophe. Write the words on the lines and add the apostrophes in the correct places.

a) Chris house has been flooded so he is staying at James Smiths house.

....

b) The waitresses tips were distributed by Alexs secretary.

....

c) As he herded them into the enclosure, the farmers sheepdog nipped at the sheeps heels.

....

6 marks

Total: _____ / 18 marks

☹ **Had a go** ☐   ☺ **Getting there** ☐   😃 **Got it!** ☐

37

Apostrophes for contraction

Teaching note: A contraction is created when two words are combined and some letters are omitted. The missing letters are indicated by an apostrophe. For example, she is → she's, where the apostrophe indicates the missing 'i' from 'is' or 'ha' from 'has'.

Challenge 1

1. Write the full form of the following contractions.

    a) haven't ....

    b) I've ....

    c) didn't ....

    d) shouldn't've ....

    e) shan't ....

    f) couldn't've ....

    g) you're ....

    h) what'll ....

    8 marks

2. Write two different full forms of the following contractions.

    a) we'd ....

    b) it'd ....

    c) she'd ....

    d) he's ....

    8 marks

38

Challenge 2

1 Complete the table.

Full forms	Contracted forms
we have	a)
b)	shouldn't
let us	c)
d)	I'd
might not	e)

5 marks

Challenge 3

1 Find the words in the passage where an apostrophe has been omitted. Write the correctly spelt words on the lines.

Wed only been gone a few minutes when the rain started.

"Isnt that just typical?" moaned Sami whod been looking forward to the picnic all day.

"Its not the end of the world," said Carrie, whos always cheerful.

"Didnt you know that theres a covered area near the swings where well be able to shelter?"

....

....

....

....

8 marks

Total: _____ / 29 marks

😐 Had a go ☐   🙂 Getting there ☐   😃 Got it! ☐

39

Using hyphens

Teaching note: Hyphens can be used to join prefixes to words and to form compound words and adjectives (e.g. quick-thinking). Sometimes, a hyphen is needed to avoid ambiguity (e.g. re-sign versus resign) or because the prefix ends in a vowel and the word begins with a vowel (e.g. re-elect).

Challenge 1

1) Match each word below with its definition.

   re-collect   recollect   re-sign   resign

Definition	Word
To announce you are leaving your job	a)
To remember	b)
To sign something again	c)
To gather things together again	d)

4 marks

2) Write a sentence for each of the hyphenated words in Question 1.

....

....

....

....

....

4 marks

40

Challenge 2

1 Use a hyphen to join each prefix to a word, then write the words on the lines below.

| de   re   ex   co   pre |
| educate   worker   employee   arranged   ice |

....

....

....

5 marks

Challenge 3

1 Find the words in each sentence that should be joined with a hyphen. Write them correctly on the line.

a) Ciara's sixteen year old sister only drinks sugar free juice.

....

b) Ben's father in law had to jump start his car.

....

c) The ex president is a superb after dinner speaker.

....

d) My hard working mum has re laid the tiles in the bathroom.

....

8 marks

Total: _____ / 21 marks

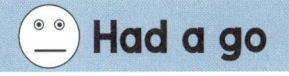

😐 Had a go ☐   🙂 Getting there ☐   😃 Got it! ☐

Adding suffixes beginning with vowels to words ending in -fer

Teaching note: When adding a suffix beginning with a vowel to a word ending in -fer, the 'r' is doubled if the syllable -fer is still stressed after the suffix is added. If the syllable is unstressed, the 'r' is not doubled.

Challenge 1

1. Add the suffixes **-ed** and **-ing** to each of the following verbs. Say the word out loud before you write it on the line. Remember the spelling rule!

   a) differ ....

   b) refer ....

   c) suffer ....

   d) prefer ....

   e) offer ....

   f) pilfer ....

   g) infer ....

   7 marks

Challenge 2

1. Select the correct spelling from the pairs of words in bold. Write the words on the lines.

   a) James attended a **conference / conferrence** about space travel.

   ....

   b) Faisal has been **transfered / transferred** to another team.

   ....

c) Isla's favourite TV series keeps **bufferring / buffering**.

....

d) The politician was **chaufferred / chauffeured** to parliament.

....

4 marks

Challenge 3

1. The following root words have had the suffixes **-ed** and **-ence** added to them. Find the new words in the word search and write them on the lines below.

| refer | infer | defer |

r	e	f	e	r	e	n	c	e	d
q	i	g	q	e	n	n	x	n	e
i	e	c	h	f	i	q	u	e	f
n	i	n	f	e	r	e	n	c	e
f	n	t	i	r	u	e	e	p	r
e	e	r	q	r	e	u	w	q	r
x	d	e	f	e	r	e	n	c	e
r	s	f	e	d	x	f	e	r	d
c	i	n	f	e	r	r	e	d	w

....

....

....

6 marks

Total: _____ / 17 marks

😐 Had a go ☐   🙂 Getting there ☐   😃 Got it! ☐

43

Dictionary skills (1)

Challenge 1

1 Write the answers to the riddles.

Use your dictionary to help you with the spelling.

a) I am a two-syllable adjective; I begin with pr and I mean valuable.

I am ....

b) I am a two-syllable verb (but I can also be a noun); I begin with d and I mean to break or spoil something.

I am ....

c) I am a four-syllable noun; I begin with bi and I am an account of someone's life, written by someone else.

I am a ....

d) I am a five-syllable adjective; I begin with a prefix that starts with 'i', and I mean between or involving different countries.

I am ....

4 marks

2 Now write your answers to Question 1 in alphabetical order.

....

....

....

....

1 mark

44

Challenge 2

1 The following tricky words have been spelt as they sound. Use your dictionary to help you spell them correctly and write them on the lines.

a) grachus ....

b) cayos ....

c) practicul ....

d) capchure ....

e) nesesary ....

f) senic ....

6 marks

Tip: A **homograph** is a word that shares the same written form as another word but has a different meaning and pronunciation. For example, wind (rhymes with kind): to wrap something like a thread or rope round several times; wind (rhymes with pinned): a current of air that moves across the Earth's surface.

Challenge 3

1 There are at least two different meanings and pronunciations for each of the following words. Write two of the different meanings on the lines.

lead a) ....

b) ....

minute c) ....

d) ....

4 marks

Total: _____ / 15 marks

😐 Had a go ☐   🙂 Getting there ☐   😀 Got it! ☐

45

Word games (2)

Challenge 1

1. Write the two words in each question that contain the same letters.

   a)   tea   pot   pat   eat   pea

   ....

   b)   riled   rifle   field   relic   filed

   ....

   c)   lance   lease   lenses   easel   sealed

   ....

   d)   scorn   shrub   shorn   brush   crush

   ....

   4 marks

Challenge 2

1. Find a four-letter word that can be made from the end of one word and the beginning of the next in each sentence below. For example,
I ma**de al**l sorts of delicious cakes for the fair. Write the word on the line.

   a)   Bren could hear church bells in the distance.

        ....

46

b) Our neighbours' dogs often bark in the night.

....

c) A shadow near the back door made me jump in fright.

....

d) The farmer's nervous mare stopped when a hare jumped out of the hedge.

....

4 marks

Challenge 3

1 Write one word that can go in front of each word in the group to make three compound words.

a)	wards	hill	cast	....
b)	cooked	stood	estimate	....
c)	hill	beat	standing	....
d)	over	roads	word	....

4 marks

2 Write two groups of your own words where one word can go in front of each to make three compound words.

a) ....

b) ....

2 marks

Total: _____ / 14 marks

😐 Had a go ☐   🙂 Getting there ☐   😃 Got it! ☐

47

Progress test 2

1. **Underline the words in the advertisement below that should have an apostrophe. Write the words on the lines and add the apostrophes in the correct places.**

   ### Happy Holidays!

   Here at Happy Holidays, we have a range of amazing offers for the holiday youve always dreamt about. Whether its zip-wiring through the trees or lying by the pool, were the answer to those dreams! Theres almost no destination we dont go to and Happy Holidays prices are so competitive, you wont look anywhere else. Read some of our customers comments below.

   Ellens comment: "Ive nothing but fantastic memories of my trip to South Africas famous wine regions!"

   Dr Rajs comment: "My wife and I hiked round Spains coast. As soon as wed finished, we booked again for next year!"

   ....

   ....

   ....

   14 marks

2. **Write these two sets of words in alphabetical order.**

   a) referred   reference   referee

   ....

   ....

   ....

48

b) deference deferring deferred

....

....

....

2 marks

3. The prefixes in the box can be joined to the words below using a hyphen. Write the hyphenated words on the lines.

anti co pre de

a) own ....

b) stress ....

c) book ....

d) freeze ....

4 marks

4. Find the incorrectly spelt words with silent letters in the passage below. Write the words correctly on the lines.

To be perfectly onest, I have very little nowledge of mountain climing. I'm much happier by the coast and ofen go to Anglesey, an iland off Wales, far away from the husle and busle of the city. Last time, I met Tim and I lisened for ours as he described his clim up Snowden and it's inspired me. Wach this space – you never now!

....

....

....

12 marks

49

5. **Add an ending that sounds like shul to change these nouns into adjectives.**

   a) residence ....

   b) substance ....

   c) torrent ....

   3 marks

6. **Unscramble the letters to complete the words in the grid that end in -ant, -ance or -ancy.**

   ceeleang   pecentxta   ntexvagatra
   ancgrafre   itanchesy   dianracy

   a) e
   b) e
   c) e
   d) f
   e) h
   f) r

   6 marks

50

7. Use your dictionary to find two different meanings for each of the following words which have two different pronunciations. Write the two different meanings on the lines.

buffet ....

....

sow ....

....

desert ....

....

6 marks

8. Write the adjectives next to their definitions.

| atrocious | conscious | malicious |

Definition	Word
When you notice or realise that something is happening.	
Describes words or actions that are intended to harm.	
Describes something very shocking or terrible.	

3 marks

Total: _____ / 50 marks

51

Words with 'ei' and 'ie'

> **Teaching note:** The spellings 'ie' and 'ei' are often used for the **ee** sound. For example, field and seize. The spelling is often 'ei' after the letter 'c'. For example, ceiling. There are, of course, lots of exceptions which just have to be learned!

Challenge 1

1 Read each word out loud, then cover, write and check. Use the second line to correct any mistakes or for extra practice. Look closely to see whether the spelling is 'ei' or 'ie'.

fierce ....

seize ....

receipt ....

belief ....

deceit ....

weird ....

6 marks

> **Tip:** The 'ei' spelling is also used in some words with an **ay** sound. For example, neighbour.

Challenge 2

1 Find the answers to the following clues.

a) A pale brown colour.

....

52

b) A deer with antlers associated with Christmas.

....

c) A piece of thin cloth that women sometimes wear over their faces.

....

d) Seventy-two divided by nine.

....

4 marks

Challenge 3

1 Unscramble the letters to find words which do not follow the 'ei' after 'c' rule.

| i s c n e c e   g e r a c l i   n c n t i a e |

....

3 marks

Total: .... / 13 marks

Had a go ☐   Getting there ☐   Got it! ☐

Adding the suffixes -ate, -ise and -ify to make verbs

Teaching note: The suffixes -ate, -ise and -ify can be used to create verbs. Sometimes these refer to making something or someone different in some way. For example, simple → simplify: to make more simple. When adding these suffixes to words ending in 'e', the 'e' is dropped.

Challenge 1

1. Add the suffix -ate or -ify to make verbs from these nouns and adjectives.

    a) sign .... b) fabric ....

    c) pure .... d) medic ....

    4 marks

Challenge 2

1. Add the suffix -ate, -ise or -ify to each of these four words.

    a) domestic .... b) solid ....

    c) intense .... d) private ....

    4 marks

2. Write the words you created in Question 1 next to the correct definitions below.

    a) To harden or set ....

    b) To bring a wild animal under control and use it as a pet ....

    c) To transfer business or industrial activities so that they are no longer under government control

    ....

    d) To make something greater in strength or amount

    ....

    4 marks

54

Challenge 3

1 The words from the box have been changed into verbs by adding the suffixes -ate, -ise or -ify. Find them in the word search and write the verbs on the lines.

| formal | class | vocal | ideal | false | origin |

e	c	i	s	e	i	f	y	j	i	i
w	e	v	e	c	b	n	c	e	a	d
q	i	v	o	c	a	l	i	s	e	e
i	e	c	h	l	i	q	u	e	a	a
f	o	r	m	a	l	i	s	e	v	l
f	n	t	i	s	u	e	e	p	i	i
e	f	a	l	s	i	f	y	q	r	s
x	d	o	r	i	g	i	n	a	t	e
r	s	f	e	f	x	f	e	r	d	c
c	i	n	f	y	r	r	e	d	w	v

....

....

....

6 marks

Total: _____ / 18 marks

Adding the suffix -en to make verbs

Teaching note: Some adjectives can be changed into verbs by simply adding the suffix -en. If the adjective ends in 'e', drop the 'e' before adding -en. For example, wide → widen; loose → loosen. For one-syllable adjectives with a short vowel sound followed by a single consonant, double the consonant before adding -en. For example, sad → sadden.

Challenge 1

1. Complete the sentences with a verb made from the adjectives below.

sweet	tight	flat	soft	ripe

   a) We had to .... our grip on Monty's lead when he saw the cat approach.

   b) Mum put the butter in the microwave to .... it.

   c) I sprinkled some sugar over the strawberries to .... them.

   d) The builder used a steamroller to .... the tarmac.

   e) Dad said we should wait another week for the apples to ....

   5 marks

56

Challenge 2

1 Solve the clues to find the verbs.

a) I am an antonym of soften.

I am ....

b) I am an antonym of lengthen.

I am ....

c) I am an antonym of to make blunt.

I am ....

d) I am an antonym of darken.

I am ....

4 marks

Challenge 3

1 Solve the clues to complete the crossword.

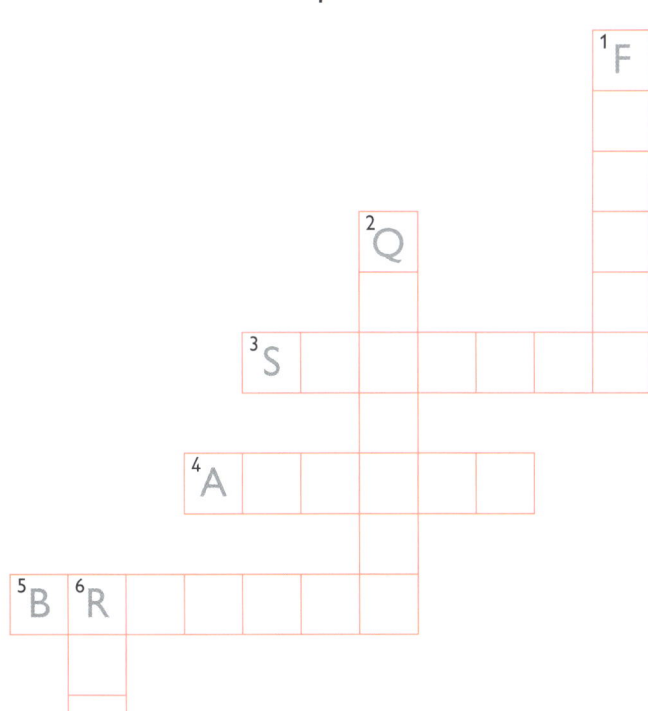

Across
3. To become tight or tense
4. To wake up
5. To become wider

Down
1. To close by means of buttons
2. To become faster
6. To flush with embarrassment

6 marks

Total: _____ / 15 marks

😐 Had a go ☐   🙂 Getting there ☐   😃 Got it! ☐

Homophones and near-homophones (1)

Teaching note: Homophones are words that sound the same as another word (or words) but have a different meaning and spelling. For example, break / brake.

Near-homophones are words that sound *almost* the same as another word but have a different meaning and spelling. For example, lose / loose.

Challenge 1

1. Select the correct homophone from the box to complete the sentences below.

| wails | guest | poor | guessed |
| routes | pour | whales | roots |

a) You can travel from Paris to Nice using two different ....

b) My little sister .... when she doesn't get her own way.

c) I .... the answer and luckily it was right!

d) The headteacher welcomed the .... to our assembly.

e) I helped Mum .... some juice for my friends.

f) Dad rescued a .... little chick that had fallen from its nest.

g) The gardener pulled the weeds up by their ....

h) On holiday, we watched some .... leaping above the sea's surface.

8 marks

58

Challenge 2

1 Write a homophone for each word below.

Word	Homophone
ball	a)
due	b)
towed	c)
place	d)
compliment	e)

5 marks

Challenge 3

1 Write a sentence for each of the following near-homophones.

> accept   except   effect   affect

....

....

....

....

....

8 marks

Total: _____ / 21 marks

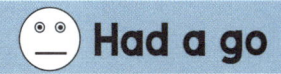

😐 Had a go ☐   🙂 Getting there ☐   😀 Got it! ☐

59

Homophones and near-homophones (2)

Challenge 1

1 Use the clues to help you write the near-homophone for each word below.

a) weary

   I am an adjective meaning cautious. ....

b) proceed

   I am a verb meaning to go in front of. ....

c) advise

   I am a noun meaning guidance in a particular situation.

   ....

3 marks

Challenge 2

1 Match these homophones with their definitions.

| desert | led | past | passed |
| dessert | lead | aisle | isle |

Definition	Word
Something sweet you might eat after a meal	a)
A soft, grey, heavy metal	b)
A long narrow gap that people can walk along between rows of seats	c)
To leave or abandon a place	d)

Definition	Word
Another word for island	e)
The past tense of the verb lead	f)
When used as a noun, this is the time before the present	g)
The past tense of the verb pass	h)

8 marks

Challenge 3

1. Underline the 15 homophones and near-homophones that have been used incorrectly in the passage. Write the correct homophones on the lines.

Olga had know idea how two brake the last part of the secret code she had found. She had bean reading it for ours and still couldn't crack it. Won minute she thought it said, "Berry this peace of paper when you have red it," the next she was shore it said, "Do knot speak allowed when you reed this." Finally, she through it aside and watched her favourite cereal on TV instead.

....

....

....

....

15 marks

Total: _____ / 26 marks

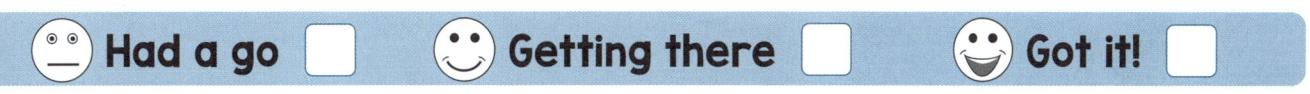

Had a go ☐   Getting there ☐   Got it! ☐

61

Dictionary skills (2)

> **Tip:** Your dictionary will tell you the word class of a word. These might be abbreviated to: verb: (v.), noun: (n.), adjective: (adj.), adverb: (adv.)

Challenge 1

1. Read the text below then use a dictionary to help you write each underlined word in the correct column in the table.

    Ronnie was <u>absolutely</u> <u>thrilled</u> that her <u>birthday</u> had <u>finally</u> arrived! She was <u>really</u> looking forward to her <u>party</u> and seeing all her <u>friends</u>. She <u>wondered</u> if she would get some <u>nice</u> presents. Last <u>year</u>, her parents had <u>presented</u> her with a <u>new</u> bike. She <u>quickly</u> <u>ran</u> downstairs into the kitchen, full of excitement. But, to her <u>complete</u> surprise, no one <u>was</u> there...

Verb (v.)	Adjective (adj.)	Noun (n.)	Adverb (adv.)

    16 marks

Challenge 2

1. Unscramble these letters to find words beginning with 'si'.

    esicnrlye   igtunsear   nsiwe   impsticlis

    ....

    ....

    4 marks

62

2 Write the words in alphabetical order.

....

....

1 mark

Challenge 3

1 Use your dictionary to help you complete the following tasks.

a) Write the noun that begins with the letters 'sp' and means a particular type of work that someone does best.

s p ....

1 mark

b) Find a word that starts with 'h' and ends with 'n' and that has no vowels.

....

1 mark

c) Find four definitions of the word 'bank'.

....

....

....

....

4 marks

Total: _____ / 27 marks

😐 Had a go ☐   🙂 Getting there ☐   😃 Got it! ☐

63

Tricky plurals

Teaching note: To form the plural of most nouns that end in 'f' or 'fe', just add an 's' at the end of the word. For example, cliff → cliffs. For some nouns that end in 'f' or 'fe', replace the 'f' or 'fe' with 'v' and add 'es'. For example, wife → wives. Some nouns that end in 'f' have plurals that can be spelt either way. For example, dwarf → dwarfs or dwarves.

Challenge 1

1. Write plural forms of each word and, if applicable, a second plural option.

Word	Plural option 1	Plural option 2
hoof		
roof		
dwarf		
waterproof		
scarf		
calf		

9 marks

Teaching note: For most words that end in a vowel followed by the letter 'o', just add 's' to make the plural. For example, kangaroo → kangaroos. If a word ends in a consonant followed by the letter 'o', the plural is sometimes formed by adding 's' and sometimes by adding 'es'. For example, piano → pianos but potato → potatoes. There is no rule for this – and some can even be spelt both ways.

Challenge 2

1. Select the correct spelling from the pairs of words in bold. Write the word on the line.

   a) Ted took some **photoes / photos** of the car.

   ....

64

b) The **echoes / echos** of the children's voices reverberated through the cave.

....

c) **Torpedoes / torpedos** are tube-shaped bombs that travel under water.

....

d) Mum picked the ripe **tomatos / tomatoes** in the greenhouse.

....

4 marks

> **Teaching note:** Some nouns do not change their spelling in the plural and some can keep the same spelling or be spelt by adding -s or -es. For example, fish / fishes. There is no rule for this – these words just have to be learned!

Challenge 3

1 Use the pictures to complete the noun phrases with the correct word.

a) A herd of ....

b) A set of ....

c) A gaggle of ....

d) A flock of ....

4 marks

Total: _____ / 17 marks

Had a go ☐   Getting there ☐   Got it! ☐

65

Word games (3)

Challenge 1

1. Find the four-letter word which can be added to the letters in capitals to make a new word to complete the sentence. Write the word you have made on the line. For example:

    The dog CERED up the bank.

    LAMB added to CERED makes CLAMBERED.

    a) Samantha LOD her head in shame. ....

    b) Uri said he would DER the parcel himself. ....

    c) The editor made a few CES to the book. ....

    d) Yolande's BED cat is unwell. ....

    4 marks

Challenge 2

1. Write one letter on each line to make four new words. The same letter must be used on both lines.

    a) mea .... able   gree .... ank

    b) stin .... ind   ran .... not

    c) stam .... ink   ram .... ain

    d) flai .... ation   pea .... ise

    4 marks

Challenge 3

1 Write 15 four-letter words using the letters in the grid. You can use any of the letters – they don't have to connect to each other.

```
M    B    F    M

R    A    S    T

C    G    P    O

N    O    T    D
```

....

....

....

....

....

15 marks

Total: _____ / 23 marks

Had a go ☐   Getting there ☐   Got it! ☐

Progress test 3

1. **Complete the word in each sentence by adding its missing silent letter and the other missing letters.**

   a) A serious illness of the lungs is called ...... n .... m o n ...... a.

   b) Our dog comes back to us when he hears the w .... s ...... l ....

   c) The climbers' a s .... of Mount Everest was a great victory.

   d) Dad c .... m l ...... picked the pie off the floor.

   4 marks

2. **Write the homophone for each word below.**

   a) sent ....

   b) pain ....

   c) rap ....

   d) bolder ....

   4 marks

3. **In each sentence below, there is a missing apostrophe and an incorrect plural. Write the two correct words on the lines.**

   a) The musical companys pianoes are made from the finest mahogany.

   ....

   b) Julia found the missing dominos in the childrens toyboxes.

   ....

68

c) Tess mum makes a wonderful shepherd's pie using her own home-grown potatos.

....

d) At eighty years of age, Kim felt she'd had a life of two halfs: the first had been a disaster but in the second she'd fulfilled her hearts desire.

....

8 marks

4. **Change the following nouns into adjectives by adding an appropriate suffix which sounds like shul.**

   a) face ....

   b) resident ....

   c) commerce ....

   d) president ....

   4 marks

5. **Add the suffix -ify or -ise to each noun below to change it into a verb.**

   a) beauty ....

   b) advert ....

   c) dignity ....

   3 marks

69

6. Write these words in alphabetical order.

> accompany   accessible
> accommodate   accordance

....

....

1 mark

7. Two words in each sentence have been spelt incorrectly.
Write the correct spellings on the line below each.

a) Althow it was late, I couldn't sleep due to my bad coff.

....

b) I haven't worn my new boots enuff so I found this morning's walk very tuff on my feet.

....

c) The storm brawt strong winds which caused the tree's bow to scratch against my window.

....

6 marks

8. **Use a hyphen to join each prefix to a word and complete the sentences.**

| co | ex | re | semi | all |
| retired | author | entered | wife | inclusive |

a) Max was the .... of a book about marine life.

b) After many years of full-time work, Hayle's mum has ....

c) Hugo .... the talent competition, confident he would make the finals this time.

d) Gryf's .... has gone to live in Iceland.

e) The Magee family were looking forward to an .... holiday in Portugal.

5 marks

Total: _____ / 35 marks

Words with unspoken sounds and syllables

> **Tip:** Watch out for tricky words that often 'lose' a sound or syllable in pronunciation. For example, desperate which is often pronounced desprate.

Challenge 1

1. Break these words up into syllables. Highlight the sound or syllable that is often 'lost'. One has been done for you.

   necessary   nec|ess|ar|y

   a) memory   ....

   b) different   ....

   c) generous   ....

   d) probably   ....

   8 marks

Challenge 2

1. These words have been written as they are often pronounced – a sound or syllable has been 'lost'. Write them correctly on the lines.

   a) accompniment ....

   b) despration   ....

   c) intrested   ....

   d) temprature   ....

   e) defnitely   ....

   f) busness   ....

   6 marks

Challenge 3

1 Use the picture clues to find words with a commonly 'lost' sound or syllable. The shaded square indicates the position of the unpronounced sound or syllable.

a)

b)

c)

d)

4 marks

Total: _____ / 18 marks

Had a go ☐   Getting there ☐   Got it! ☐

Prefixes

> **Teaching note**
>
> A prefix is a letter or letters that can be added to the beginning of a word to change its meaning. For example, tidy → untidy.
>
> An antonym is a word that has an opposite meaning to another word. For example, hot → cold.
>
> Sometimes, adding a prefix can give an opposite meaning. For example, appear → disappear.

Challenge 1

1. Select the correct prefix from the box to create an antonym for each of the following words.

   | im   in   il   ir   dis   un |

   a) familiar ....
   b) regular ....
   c) satisfaction ....
   d) complete ....
   e) legal ....
   f) practical ....
   g) appreciative ....
   h) relevant ....
   i) credulous ....
   j) sincere ....

   10 marks

Challenge 2

1. a) Write the word from below that is a noun. Use your dictionary to help you if you are not sure.

   substandard   submarine   submerge

   ....

   1 mark

74

b) Write the word with the prefix anti- that is an adjective.

anticlockwise   antidote   antifreeze

....

1 mark

2 Write two sentences containing the words you wrote in Question 1.

....

....

....

....

4 marks

Challenge 3

1 Unscramble the letters to find words that start with a prefix.

a) u r e n s u   ....

b) r a t e h e   ....

c) m e a r i s h   ....

d) d p n t i s a p o i   ....

e) s g n i i f i c a i n n t   ....

5 marks

Total: _____ / 21 marks

Had a go ☐   Getting there ☐   Got it! ☐

75

Word families

Teaching note: Words with the same root can be grouped into word families. For example, sign, signify, signature. This can help you work out the meaning of new words and help with their spelling.

Challenge 1

1. Write six words that start with the prefix auto. Use your dictionary if you need help.

   ....

   ....

   ....

   6 marks

Challenge 2

1. Write the three-letter root word that is in each word in this word family.

   | television   invisible   visibility   visual |

   ....

   1 mark

2. Circle the word below that is the meaning of the root word from Question 1.

   disappear   distant   faint   see

   1 mark

76

Challenge 3

1 Group the words that are a family and write them in the tables to show their different word classes. Some words might have more than one word class option. Use your dictionary to help you.

> pitiful　　cleaner　　breath　　pity　　unclean
> breathe　　pitiable　　breathless　　cleanly
> breathlessly　　pitiably　　clean　　cleanliness

Word class	Word family
Noun	
Adjective	
Verb	
Adverb	

Word class	Word family
Noun	
Adjective	
Verb	
Adverb	

Word class	Word family
Noun	
Adjective	
Verb	
Adverb	

15 marks

Total: _____ / 23 marks

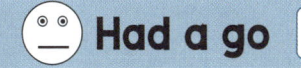

Had a go ☐　　Getting there ☐　　Got it! ☐

Dictionary skills (3)

Challenge 1

1 a) Write these words in alphabetical order.

        wretched   wreath   wreckage

....

1 mark

b) Write a definition for each word.

....

....

....

3 marks

Challenge 2

1 Use your dictionary to help you answer the following.

a) In which sport would you use a puck?

....

b) What does an ornithologist do?

....

c) Write three ingredients you would find in gazpacho.

....

d) Find three words that begin with the letter 'x'.

....

4 marks

Teaching note: A synonym is a word with the same or similar meaning as another word. For example, neat → tidy.

Challenge 3

1. Use a thesaurus to find a synonym and an antonym for each given word.

	Synonym	Word	Antonym
a)		stop	
b)		morning	
c)		loud	
d)		near	
e)		buy	

10 marks

2. Find the six words that Gretchen has spelt incorrectly. Write them on the lines below.

Hi Gisela!

Having a great time here in Hungry. There is so much to do. I've been white-water wrafting and zip-wyring already! Dad is going to sky-dive tomorrow – can you belive he will be jumping out of a plane with a parashoot?

Hope you are well and you have recovered from the flew.

Love Gretchen x

....

....

6 marks

Total: _____ / 24 marks

Had a go ☐ Getting there ☐ Got it! ☐

Tricky words (1)

Tip: Some words are tricky to spell because they don't follow the spelling or phoneme rules you have learned. Breaking the words into syllables can help you learn to spell them. For example, prop-er-ly.

Challenge 1

1. Read each word out loud, then cover, write and check. Use the second line to correct any mistakes or for extra practice.

frequently ....

nuisance ....

sufficient ....

category ....

awkward ....

convenience ....

twelfth ....

vehicle ....

sincerely ....

exaggerate ....

conscience ....

guarantee ....

12 marks

Challenge 2

1 Write five words that belong with convenience in a word family.

....

....

....

5 marks

Challenge 3

1 Complete the grid by answering the clues. The answers are words that can be found in Challenge 1.

    a) To suggest that something is worse, better or more important than it really is

    b) Enough for the purpose

    c) Three behind fifteenth

    d) Embarrassing and difficult to deal with

a)
b)
c)
d)

4 marks

2 The letters in the shaded squares can be rearranged to make another word (which isn't on the Challenge 1 list). Write the word on the line below.

....

1 mark

Total: _____ / 22 marks

Had a go ☐   Getting there ☐   Got it! ☐

81

Tricky words (2)

Challenge 1

1. Read each word out loud, then cover, write and check. Use the second line to correct any mistakes or for extra practice.

bargain ....

cemetery ....

embarrass ....

environment ....

marvellous ....

amateur ....

controversy ....

recognise ....

hindrance ....

stomach ....

rhythm ....

yacht ....

12 marks

Challenge 2

1 Add a suffix to each word below to change them into adjectives.

> environment   controversy   embarrass

....

....

3 marks

2 Write a sentence containing each adjective you have made.

a) ....

b) ....

c) ....

6 marks

Challenge 3

1 The answers to the following clues are words in Challenge 1.

a) Someone who does something, such as sport, for a hobby, not a job.

....

b) Something that makes it more difficult for you to do something.

....

c) A lot of discussion and argument about something.

....

3 marks

Total: _____ / 24 marks

Had a go ☐   **Getting there** ☐   **Got it!** ☐

Tricky words (3)

Challenge 1

1. Read each word out loud, then cover, write and check. Use the second line to correct any mistakes or for extra practice.

committee ....

appreciate ....

bruise ....

conscious ....

symbol ....

forty ....

recommend ....

7 marks

Challenge 2

1. Complete each sentence with an appropriate form of the words below.

| symbol | immediate | interrupt |

a) Tia welcomed the ....to the history lesson.

b) "Line up ....," said the teacher.

c) The lighting of the Olympic torch .... peace and friendship.

3 marks

84

Challenge 3

1 Answer the clues to complete the crossword. The answers to the clues are words in Challenge 1.

Across
1. A shape or a design that stands for or represents something
3. A group of people who meet to make decisions
4. To tell other people that someone or something is good
5. To like something for its good qualities

Down
2. An injury that appears as a purple mark on your body
3. When you are aware of something happening

6 marks

Total: _____ / 16 marks

Had a go ☐   Getting there ☐   Got it! ☐

85

Word games (4)

Challenge 1

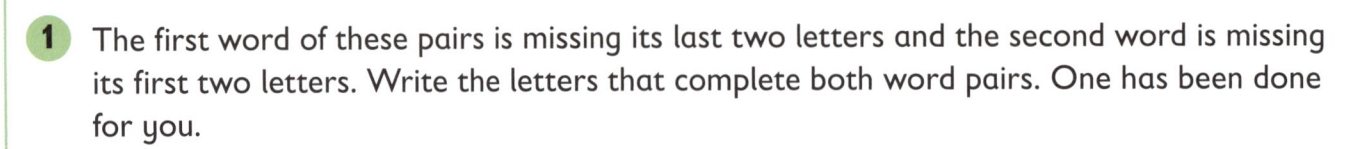

1. The first word of these pairs is missing its last two letters and the second word is missing its first two letters. Write the letters that complete both word pairs. One has been done for you.

   | o | p | **e** | **n** | j | o | y |

   a) | s | y | r | _ | _ | o | n |

   b) | c | r | u | n | _ | _ | u | n | k |

   c) | b | r | e | a | d | _ | _ | i | r | t | y |

   d) | b | u | t | t | _ | _ | w | a | r | d |

   4 marks

2. The letters in the shaded squares make a five-letter word. Write the word on the line below.

   ....

   1 mark

Challenge 2

1. Crack the codes!

   a) If the code for STIRRED is 3456678, what is 45678 the code for?

   ....

86

b) If the code for WRECKAGE is 98754327, what is 93278 the code for?

....

c) If the code for CHALLENGE is 381225795, what is 17952 the code for?

....

3 marks

Challenge 3

1 Find the three-letter word which can be added to the letters in capitals to make a complete word, without changing the order of the letters. Write the word you have made on the line below each.

For example:

The little boat was FLING on the water.

OAT added to FLING makes FLOATING.

a) The TISTS spent a lot of money in Paris.

....

b) Chen couldn't COMPRED what Li was saying.

....

c) Ishana likes driving in the COUNSIDE.

....

d) Hanna is RENED for her ability to look on the bright side.

....

4 marks

Total: _____ / 12 marks

Had a go ☐   Getting there ☐   Got it! ☐

Progress test 4

1. **Use a dictionary to find the definition and word class for each word.**

	Word	Definition	Class
a)	guarantor		
b)	controversy		
c)	conscientious		
d)	sincerely		
e)	hinder		

10 marks

2. **Unscramble the letters to find words that start with a prefix.**

| icantepist | ismnedlha | ilarepcerleab |

....

3 marks

3. **Add the suffix -ify, -en or -ise to each noun below to change it into a verb.**

a) thick ....

b) priority ....

c) terror ....

3 marks

88

4. There are missing apostrophes in two contractions in each sentence.
Write the words with the correctly placed apostrophes on the lines below each.

a) Ive been looking for that book for ages and its been under my bed all this time!

   ....

b) Theres no time to lose! If we dont catch the 8:10am bus, we will miss our train.

   ....

c) Bernie couldntve studied any harder but hes just found out he failed the test.

   ....

   6 marks

5. Choose the correct spelling of the words in bold.
Write the correct word on the line below each sentence.

a) Mel is feeling very tired as she comes to the end of her **pregnancy / pregnency**.

   ....

b) The politician's **incompetance / incompetence** was headline news.

   ....

c) The nurse used **disinfectant / disinfectent** to clean the cut.

   ....

   3 marks

89

6. Choose the correct word from the box to complete each sentence.

| pretentious | nutritious | cautious | superstitious |

a) Be very .... when crossing that busy road.

b) Maya always brings a very .... packed lunch to school.

c) I've always thought that television celebrity was a bit

....

d) Matt, who is very ...., believes black cats are lucky.

4 marks

7. Unscramble these words which have the letter string 'ough'.

| g b o u o r h   h b g o u   h a h u l t o g |

....

....

....

3 marks

90

8. **Find the words that are missing their silent letters and write them correctly on the lines below each sentence.**

   a)   The firefihters pulled the survivors from the reckage of the car crash.

   ………………………………………………   ………………………………………………………

   b)   The thisle is one of Scotland's best-nown symbols.

   ………………………………………………   ………………………………………………………

   c)   Ollie tried to convince us that he had seen a gost emerging from the tom.

   ………………………………………………   ………………………………………………………

   6 marks

9. **Seven homophones have been used incorrectly in the passage below. Write them correctly on the lines.**

   Finally, they're was a paws in my baby brother's balling. I blue on his head which made him laugh, then I red him a storey about a little bird that flue away from its nest but came back when it was hungry.

   ………………………………   ………………………………………   ………………………………………

   ………………………………   ………………………………………   ………………………………………

   ………………………………………

   7 marks

   Total: _____ / 45 marks

91

Answers

Pages 6–11

1. a) Mum's, tooth's   b) Philippa's, Bill's
   c) It's, we'll   d) Ashrif's, boys' **[8]**
2. a) politician   b) condition   c) confession
   d) injection   e) extension   f) magician **[6]**
3. a) mist   b) missed   c) berry   d) bury **[4]**
4. a) hungrily   b) finally   c) simply **[3]**
5. a) We've, he's   b) shan't, It's
   c) There's, can't   d) Dad's, it'll **[8]**
6. a) regularly   b) possibly   c) nastily   d) gently **[4]**
7. a) superstar   b) autopilot
   c) submerge   d) antiseptic **[4]**
8. **Apostrophe to show a contraction:** We've, It's, She's, we'd, She'd; **Apostrophe to show possession:** Mum's, area's, Mum's, sister's, Dad's **[10]**
9. a) preparation   b) condemnation
   c) sensation   d) assignation **[4]**
10. a) courageous   b) vigorous
    c) courteous   d) humorous **[4]**
11. a) antique   b) unique   c) tongue **[3]**
12. a) Invasion   b) division   c) collision **[3]**
13. a) forgotten   b) preferred   c) beginning **[3]**

Pages 12–13

Challenge 1
1. Answers will vary. **[1]**

Challenge 2
1. a) delicious   b) precious
   c) vicious   d) gracious **[4]**

Challenge 3
1. Answers will vary. **[5]**

Pages 14–15

Challenge 1
1. a) in|fec|tious   b) cau|tious
   c) nu|tri|tious   d) fic|ti|tious **[4]**

Challenge 2
1. a) fictitious   b) cautious   c) ambitious
   d) nutritious   e) infectious **[5]**

Challenge 3
1. fractious, scrumptious, pretentious. Definitions will vary. **[6]**

Pages 16–17

Challenge 1
1. a) artificial   b) special   c) substantial
   d) partial   e) essential **[5]**

Challenge 2
1. a) facial   b) commercial
   c) social   d) confidential **[4]**

Challenge 3
1. a) glacial   b) beneficial
   c) racial; Sentences will vary. **[9]**

Pages 18–19

Challenge 1
1. a) disturbance   b) tolerant
   c) observant   d) guidance **[4]**

Challenge 2
1. a) hesitancy   b) reassurance   c) vacancy
   d) instance   e) reluctant   f) occupant **[6]**

Challenge 3
1. pregnant, substance, redundant, infancy, reassurance, expectance **[6]**

Pages 20–21

Challenge 1
1. a) frequent   b) intelligent   c) dominant
   d) recent   e) occupant   f) assistant **[6]**

Challenge 2
1. competence/competency, confidence, transparency, eloquence/eloquency **[4]**

Challenge 3
1. a) emergent   b) violent
   c) fluent; Sentences will vary. **[9]**

Pages 22–23

Challenge 1
1. a) horrible   b) adorable
   c) sensible   d) applicable **[4]**

Challenge 2
1. a) noticeable   b) impossible
   c) changeable   d) visible **[4]**

Challenge 3
1. a) possible   b) understandable
   c) sensible   d) dependable **[4]**

Pages 24–25

Challenge 1
1. conceivably, unforgettably, noticeably, agreeably **[4]**

Challenge 2
1. a) variably   b) reliably   c) pitiably   d) deniably **[4]**

Challenge 3
1. a) visibly   b) incredibly   c) knowledgeably
   d) changeably   e) irreplaceably   f) horribly **[6]**

2. changeably, horribly, incredibly, irreplaceably, knowledgeably, visibly **[1]**

Pages 26–27
Challenge 1
1. Two words from:
   a) in, era, opera, able, nope, per
   b) port, nit, it, unit, unity, tun   c) hind, ran, an, in, hi
   d) met, meter, me **[8]**

Challenge 2
1. a) cold, four   b) sold, paid   c) edge, pith
   d) hose, suit   e) limb, care **[10]**

Challenge 3
1. a) weekend   b) waterfall
   c) carpark   d) suitcase **[4]**
2. a) live   b) stink   c) lots **[3]**

Pages 28–31
1. a) caution, cautious   b) space, spacious
   c) fiction, fictitious   d) repetition, repetitious **[8]**
2. a) reassurance   b) occupant   c) vacancy **[3]**
3. a) innocence   b) frequency   c) confidence **[3]**
4. a) official   b) commercial
   c) partial   d) essential **[4]**
5. a) suspicious   b) ferocious
   c) gracious; Sentences will vary. **[9]**
6. 1. official   2. assurance   3. vacancy
   4. nutritious   5. frequency   6. malicious
   7. beneficial   8. ambitious **[8]**

Pages 32–33
Challenge 1
1. Answers will vary. **[1]**

Challenge 2
1. a) rough, though   b) bought, tough
   c) plough, troughs   d) enough, cough **[8]**

Challenge 3
1. **long o sound:** although, dough, though
   aw sound: brought, thought, fought, bought, ought
   uff sound: enough, tough
   off sound: trough, cough
   ow sound: bough, plough **[14]**

Pages 34–35
Challenge 1
1. a) rhombus   b) comb   c) knuckle   d) gnome **[4]**

Challenge 2
1. autumn, island, halfway, sandwiches, calves, talked **[6]**

Challenge 3
1. a) whistle   b) ascent   c) receipt **[3]**

Pages 36–37
Challenge 1
1. a) men's, coach's   b) prince's, castle's
   c) children's, park keeper's   d) Brittany's, gran's **[8]**

Challenge 2
1. boys', child's, company's, Arkwrights' **[4]**

Challenge 3
1. a) Chris' / Chris's, James Smith's
   b) waitresses', Alex's   c) farmer's, sheep's **[6]**

Pages 38–39
Challenge 1
1. a) have not   b) I have   c) did not
   d) should not have   e) shall not
   f) could not have   g) you are   h) what will **[8]**
2. a) we had, we would   b) it had, it would
   c) she had, she would   d) he is, he has **[8]**

Challenge 2
1. a) we've   b) should not   c) let's
   d) I would / I had   e) mightn't **[5]**

Challenge 3
1. We'd, Isn't, who'd, It's, who's, Didn't, there's, we'll **[8]**

Pages 40–41
Challenge 1
1. a) resign   b) recollect   c) re-sign   d) re-collect **[4]**
2. Answers will vary. **[4]**

Challenge 2
1. de-ice, re-educate, ex-employee, co-worker, pre-arranged **[5]**

Challenge 3
1. a) sixteen-year-old, sugar-free
   b) father-in-law, jump-start
   c) ex-president, after-dinner
   d) hard-working, re-laid **[8]**

Pages 42–43
Challenge 1
1. a) differed, differing   b) referred, referring
   c) suffered, suffering   d) preferred, preferring
   e) offered, offering   f) pilfered, pilfering
   g) inferred, inferring **[7]**

Challenge 2
1. a) conference   b) transferred
   c) buffering   d) chauffeured **[4]**

Challenge 3
1. referred, reference, deference, deferred, inferred, inference **[6]**

93

Pages 44–45
Challenge 1
1. a) precious/priceless b) damage
   c) biography d) international **[4]**
2. biography, damage, international, precious/priceless **[1]**

Challenge 2
1. a) gracious b) chaos c) practical
   d) capture e) necessary f) scenic **[6]**

Challenge 3
1. Answers will vary. Examples:
   a) To go in front of
   b) A soft, grey, heavy metal
   c) A measurement of time/a sixtieth of an hour
   d) Very tiny amount **[4]**

Pages 46–47
Challenge 1
1. a) tea, eat b) field, filed
   c) lease, easel d) shrub, brush **[4]**

Challenge 2
1. a) arch b) soft c) down d) rest **[4]**

Challenge 3
1. a) down b) under c) up d) cross **[4]**
2. Answers will vary. **[2]**

Pages 48–51
1. you've, it's, we're, There's, don't, Holidays', won't, customers', Ellen's, I've, Africa's, Raj's, Spain's, we'd **[14]**
2. a) referee, reference, referred
   b) deference, deferred, deferring **[2]**
3. a) co-own b) de-stress c) pre-book
   d) anti-freeze **[4]**
4. honest, knowledge, climbing, often, island, hustle, bustle, listened, hours, climb, watch, know **[12]**
5. a) residential b) substantial c) torrential **[3]**
6. a) elegance b) expectant c) extravagant
   d) fragrance e) hesitancy f) radiancy **[6]**
7. Answers will vary. **[6]**
8. a) conscious b) malicious c) atrocious **[3]**

Pages 52–53
Challenge 1
1. Words spelt correctly **[6]**

Challenge 2
1. a) beige b) reindeer c) veil d) eight **[4]**

Challenge 3
1. science, glacier, ancient **[3]**

Pages 54–55
Challenge 1
1. a) signify b) fabricate c) purify
   d) medicate **[4]**

Challenge 2
1. a) domesticate b) solidify
   c) intensify d) privatise **[4]**
2. a) solidify b) domesticate
   c) privatise d) intensify **[4]**

Challenge 3
1. formalise, classify, vocalise, idealise, falsify, originate **[6]**

Pages 56–57
Challenge 1
1. a) tighten b) soften c) sweeten
   d) flatten e) ripen **[5]**

Challenge 2
1. a) harden b) shorten c) sharpen d) lighten **[4]**

Challenge 3
1. 1. fasten 2. quicken 3. stiffen
   4. awaken 5. broaden 6. redden **[6]**

Pages 58–59
Challenge 1
1. a) routes b) wails c) guessed d) guest
   e) pour f) poor g) roots h) whales **[8]**

Challenge 2
1. a) bawl b) dew c) toad / toed
   d) plaice e) complement **[5]**

Challenge 3
1. Answers will vary. **[8]**

Pages 60–61
Challenge 1
1. a) wary b) precede c) advice **[3]**

Challenge 2
1. a) dessert b) lead c) aisle d) desert
   e) isle f) led g) past h) passed **[8]**

Challenge 3
1. know/no, two/to, brake/break, bean/been, ours/hours, Won/One, Berry/Bury, peace/piece, red/read, shore/sure, knot/not, allowed/aloud, reed/read, through/threw, cereal/serial **[15]**

Pages 62–63

Challenge 1

1. **Verb:** wondered, presented, ran, was
   Adjective: thrilled, nice, new, complete
   Noun: birthday, party, friends, year
   Adverb: absolutely, finally, really, quickly **[16]**

Challenge 2

1. sincerely, signature, sinew, simplistic **[4]**
2. signature, simplistic, sincerely, sinew **[1]**

Challenge 3

1. a) speciality/specialism **[1]**   b) hymn **[1]**
   c) Answers will vary. Examples: The raised area along the edge of a river or canal. A group or line of something such as machines. To tilt or tip, for example when an airplane changes direction. To deposit money in a bank. **[4]**

Pages 64–65

Challenge 1

1. hoofs, hooves; roofs; dwarfs, dwarves; waterproofs; scarfs, scarves; calves **[9]**

Challenge 2

1. a) photos   b) echoes
   c) torpedoes   d) tomatoes **[4]**

Challenge 3

1. a) deer   b) knives   c) geese   d) sheep **[4]**

Pages 66–67

Challenge 1

1. a) low**er**ed   b) de**liv**er
   c) **chang**es   d) be**lov**ed **[4]**

Challenge 2

1. a) meat, table, greet, tank   b) stink, kind, rank, knot
   c) stamp, pink, ramp, pain   d) flair, ration, pear, rise **[4]**

Challenge 3

1. Answers will vary. **[15]**

Pages 68–71

1. a) pneumonia   b) whistle   c) ascent   d) calmly **[4]**
2. a) scent   b) pane   c) wrap   d) boulder **[4]**
3. a) company's, pianos   b) dominoes, children's
   c) Tess' / Tess's, potatoes   d) halves, heart's **[8]**
4. a) facial   b) residential
   c) commercial   d) presidential **[4]**
5. a) beautify   b) advertise   c) dignify **[3]**
6. accessible, accommodate, accompany, accordance **[1]**
7. a) although, cough   b) enough, tough
   c) brought, bough **[6]**
8. a) co-author   b) semi-retired   c) re-entered
   d) ex-wife   e) all-inclusive **[5]**

Pages 72–73

Challenge 1

1. a) mem|or|y   b) dif|fer|ent
   c) gen|er|ous   d) pro|ba|bly **[8]**

Challenge 2

1. a) accompaniment   b) desperation
   c) interested   d) temperature
   e) definitely   f) business **[6]**

Challenge 3

1. a) vegetables   b) chocolate
   c) restaurant   d) temperature **[4]**

Pages 74–75

Challenge 1

1. a) unfamiliar   b) irregular
   c) dissatisfaction   d) incomplete
   e) illegal   f) impractical
   g) unappreciative   h) irrelevant
   i) incredulous   j) insincere **[10]**

Challenge 2

1. a) submarine **[1]**   b) anticlockwise **[1]**
2. Sentences will vary. **[4]**

Challenge 3

1. a) unsure   b) reheat   c) mishear
   d) disappoint   e) insignificant **[5]**

Pages 76–77

Challenge 1

1. Answers will vary. **[6]**

Challenge 2

1. vis **[1]**   2. see **[1]**

Challenge 3

1.

Word class	Word family
Noun	pity
Adjective	pitiable, pitiful
Verb	pity
Adverb	pitiably

Word class	Word family
Noun	cleaner, cleanliness, clean
Adjective	clean, unclean, cleaner
Verb	clean
Adverb	cleanly, clean

95

Word class	Word family
Noun	breath
Adjective	breathless
Verb	breathe
Adverb	breathlessly

[15]

Pages 78–79
Challenge 1
1. a) wreath, wreckage, wretched **[1]**
   b) Answers will vary. **[3]**

Challenge 2
1. a) ice hockey b) studies birds
   c) Any three from: tomatoes, peppers, cucumbers, red onion, garlic
   d) Answers will vary. **[4]**

Challenge 3
1. Answers will vary. Examples:
   a) halt, go   b) dawn, night
   c) noisy, quiet d) close, far
   e) purchase, sell **[10]**
2. Hungary, rafting, wiring, believe, parachute, flu **[6]**

Pages 80–81
Challenge 1
1. Words spelt correctly. **[12]**

Challenge 2
1. Answers will vary. Examples: convenient, conveniently, inconvenient, inconveniently, inconvenience. **[5]**

Challenge 3
1. a) exaggerate b) sufficient
   c) twelfth   d) awkward **[4]**
2. laugh **[1]**

Pages 82–83
Challenge 1
1. Words spelt correctly **[12]**

Challenge 2
1. environmental, controversial, embarrassing / embarrassed **[3]**
2. Answers will vary. **[6]**

Challenge 3
1. a) amateur b) hindrance c) controversy **[3]**

Pages 84–85
Challenge 1
1. Words spelt correctly. **[7]**

Challenge 2
1. a) interruption b) immediately
   c) symbolises/symbolised **[3]**

Challenge 3
1. 1. symbol   2. bruise
   3. committee (across), conscious (down)
   4. recommend   5. appreciate **[6]**

Pages 86–87
Challenge 1
1. a) syrup upon   b) crunch chunk
   c) breadth thirty d) button onward **[4]**
2. touch **[1]**

Challenge 2
1. a) TIRED b) WAGER c) ANGEL **[3]**

Challenge 3
1. a) tourists   b) comprehend
   c) countryside   d) renowned **[4]**

Pages 88–91
1. Word classes:
   a) noun b) noun c) adjective
   d) adverb e) verb; Definitions will vary. **[10]**
2. antiseptic, mishandle, irreplaceable **[3]**
3. a) thicken b) prioritise
   c) terrorise / terrify **[3]**
4. a) I've, it's b) There's, don't
   c) couldn't've, he's **[6]**
5. a) pregnancy b) incompetence
   c) disinfectant **[3]**
6. a) cautious   b) nutritious
   c) pretentious d) superstitious **[4]**
7. borough, bough, although **[3]**
8. a) firefighters, wreckage b) thistle, known
   c) ghost, tomb **[6]**
9. they're/there, paws/pause, balling/bawling, blue/blew, red/read, storey/story, flue/flew **[7]**